I0817245

Mindfulness JOURNAL

PENGUIN BOOKS

PENGUIN BOOKS

Penguin Books is part of the Penguin Random House group of companies whose addresses can be found at global.penguinrandomhouse.com

Published by Penguin Random House SEA Pte Ltd
40 Penjuru Lane, #03-12, Block 2
Singapore 609216

First published in Penguin Books by Penguin Random House SEA 2025

Content credit: Henu Mehtani
Designer credit: Sunayana Dey

1 0 9 8 7 6 5 4 3 2 1

ISBN: 9789815323375

Printed at Thomson Press India Ltd, New Delhi

www.penguin.sg

This journal belongs to:

Nature Explorer

I find a cozy spot outside. I close my eyes, and get ready for a nature adventure.

I listen for sounds like ____________________

____

I sniff to smell the ____________________

____

I feel on my skin ____________________

____

____

____

I open my eyes and look for something new in nature—maybe ________________________________

____

____

____

____

I notice the colors and shapes of what I see

____

____

____

I take a deep breath in through my nose, and slowly exhale through my mouth.

My morning begins with a big, bright smile.

My smile makes others smile too. It gets passed on to ______________________________

____

____

I think that ______________________________
has a beautiful smile because

____

____

____

I can start a Smile Club by bringing together ______________________,
wearing ______________, and spreading joy wherever we go.

Draw or paste a picture of you smiling ear to ear.

Bend and Up

I give my toes a high-five, give my ears a hand rub. Then I repeat and repeat.
After this super-friendly meet-and-greet:

My toes feel like ____________________

____

____

____

____

My ears feel like ____________________

____

____

____

____

My breath feels like ______________________________

____

____

____

____

After the 'Bend and Up' exercise, my body feels like ______________________________________

____

____

____

After the 'Bend and Up' exercise, my mind feels like ______________________________________

____

____

____

This super-session usually lasts for ______________ minutes.

Zoomin' to the Sky

- It is me soaring through the air on a swing.

- When I swing high up, it feels like I am on

Cloud seven

Cloud five

Cloud nine

Imagine and draw your happy self, soaring through the sky, enjoying every moment of your swing ride.

Cloud Creation

As I relax in the coziest hammock, gently swaying between the vibrant ends of a rainbow, I spot a cloud.

Draw the cloud's playful shape; it could be an animal, a toy, a bird, a person, or anything you find fun.

Ninja Poses

It's time to wake up my inner ninja. I am strong, powerful, and unstoppable.

Count your deep breaths like a ninja, and every time you reach five, strike a silent ninja karate pose. Repeat until you have done all the poses.
Be careful while doing the poses.

Hand Power

I take deep breaths using my hand.

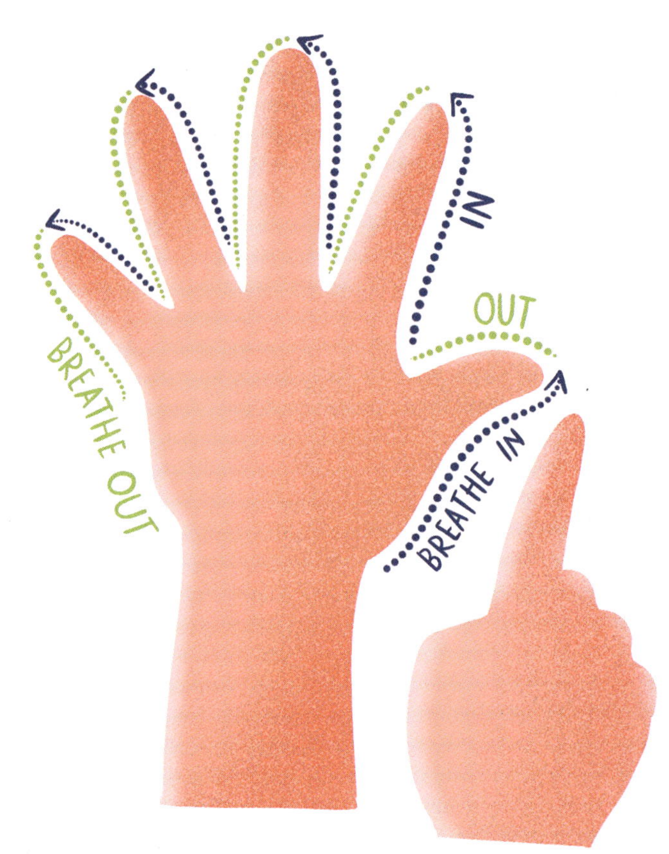

*Place your hand on the grid,
then breathe while your finger follows the movement
around your hand.*

Breathe In, Breathe Out

My three mega-powerful inhales and exhales.

I inhale to the count of ____________________

I hold to the count of ______________________

I exhale to the count of ____________________

It takes me _______ minutes to do this activity.

It makes me feel ___________________________

____

I do this daily in the:

- [ ] morning
- [ ] afternoon
- [ ] evening

____

____

____

____

____

____

Write your morning routine.

Body Clues

I can sense where emotions arise within my body.

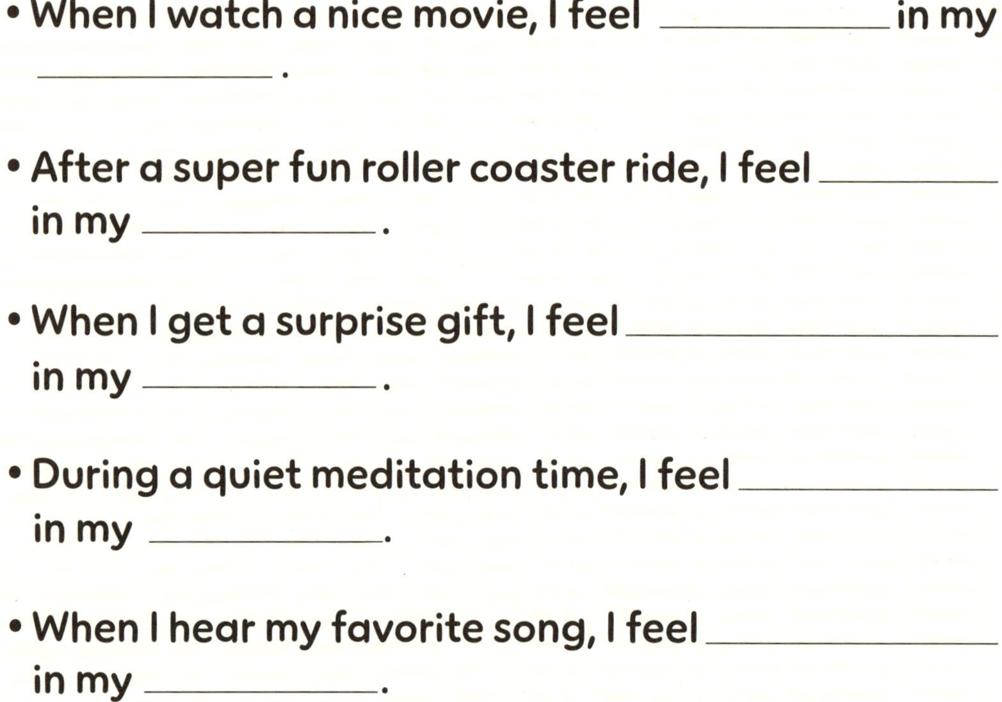

- When I watch a nice movie, I feel ____________ in my ____________.
- After a super fun roller coaster ride, I feel ____________ in my ____________.
- When I get a surprise gift, I feel ____________ in my ____________.
- During a quiet meditation time, I feel ____________ in my ____________.
- When I hear my favorite song, I feel ____________ in my ____________.

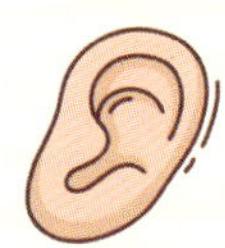

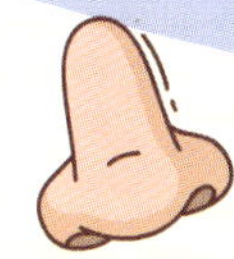

Also,

- When I am alone at night, I feel ______________________ in my ______________.
- If I skip meals for a while, I feel ______________________ in my ______________.
- After my legs hang from a chair for a long time, I feel ______________ in my legs.
- If I am not ready for a test, I feel ______________________ in my ______________.
- When I see my friend sad, I feel ______________________ in my ______________.

My People

I love them the most.

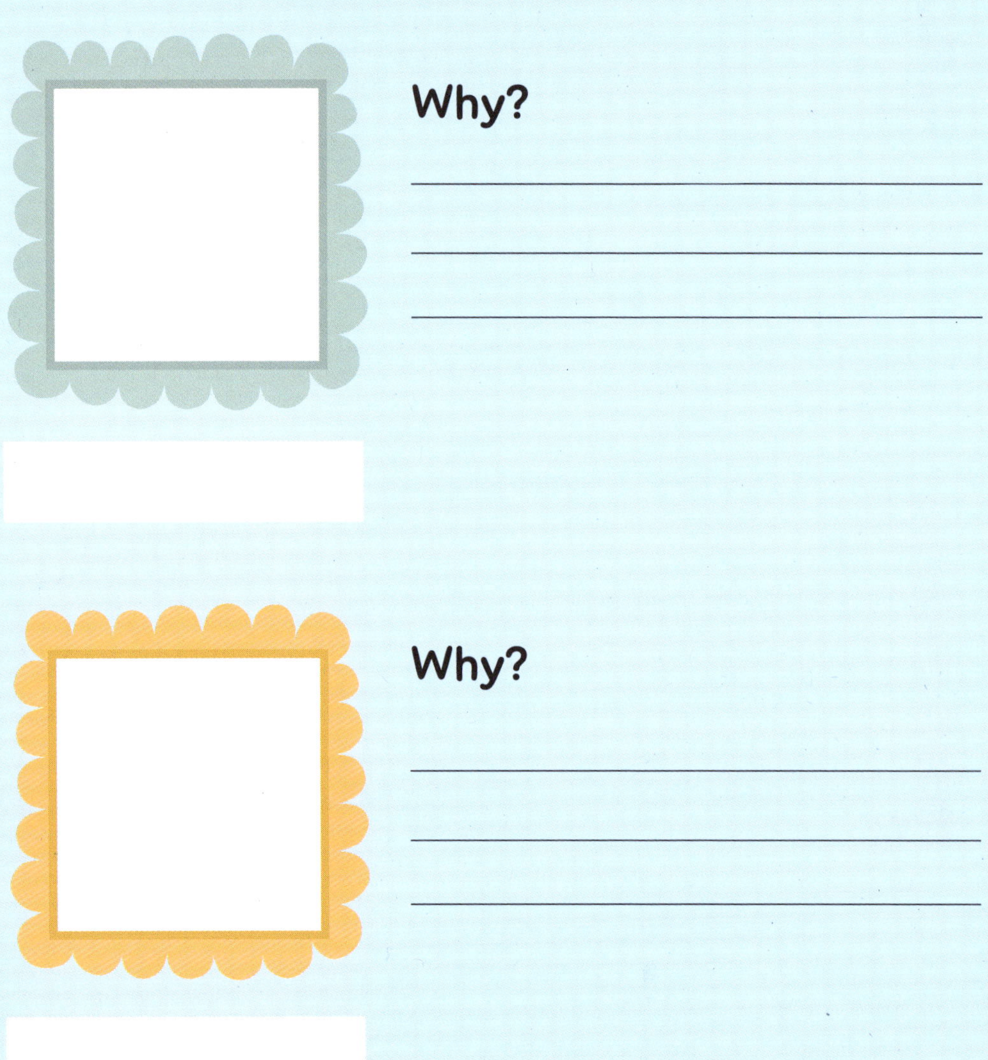

Why?

Why?

Feel the Color

Colorful things I spot around me.

Red	White	Blue

Black	Purple	Orange

Brown	Yellow	Green

The colors bring out a whole bunch of emotions.

Fill in the emotions that evoke with each color.

My Typical Day

The moment I wake up, I ______________________________

As night falls, I am back in bed, getting ready for yet another day ahead.

Share your daily routine, from the moment you wake up until bedtime.

These things remind me of:

A bright yellow flower ______________________________

____

A gray sky ______________________________

____

Hot cocoa ______________________________

____

Twinkling stars ______________________________

____

Ocean waves ______________________________

____

Fluffy white cloud ______________________________

____

Beach sand ______________________________

____

Freshly baked cookies ______________________________

____

Colorful balloons in the sky ______________________________

____

Rain tapping on window ______________________________

____

____

Breakfast flavors

My morning meal that I ate heartily.

Draw what you ate. List every flavor you tasted and describe how each made you feel.

My Uplifting Mantra

I am strong, I am brave,
and I will give my best.
With a happy heart,
I will face every test.

Repeat this mantra aloud eleven times daily for an extra boost.

Write an uplifting mantra for yourself.
Record it in your own voice.
When you face challenges, close your eyes, play this mantra,
and feel the instant cheer.

Gratitude Sparks

Ten blessings that bring me joy and gratitude.

Take a moment to think and write about the wonderful things in your life. Feel blessed!

To-do

I am jotting down my present tasks and priorities.

Rolling Tears

Ah, that instance...
I did not feel like being seen.
I hid under my blanket as tears rolled down my cheeks.

Here is what happened:

gave me a bear hug.

Shhh... Listen Up

I tune in to the sounds around me.

For two minutes, close your eyes and listen around.
Jot down or doodle the feelings these sounds evoke within you.

Dream Replay

My latest dream!
Here, I bring it to life.

Draw a colorful doodle that tells the story of your dream, and how it made you feel.

Ray by Ray Affirmations

As I draw sunrays, I write affirmations on each to share with the universe.

Affirmations are powerful, positive statements. Make it a habit to write one each day, and always remember to be kind to yourself.

Spot On

What Do I See?

Quickly look around and draw three things that you see.

Now, let's zoom in! Write three fun details about each of them.

I Crafted Taste

My ice cream is a hit— wanna know how?
Licks bring joy, and folks say, 'Wow!'

Flavor name:

Ingredients:

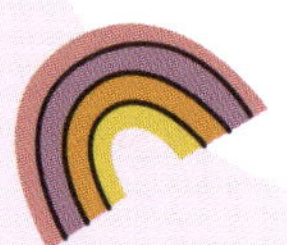

Tastes like:

Magic in each bite:

Invent your own unique ice cream flavor. Give a name to it, list the ingredients, what it tastes like, and what makes it extraordinary.

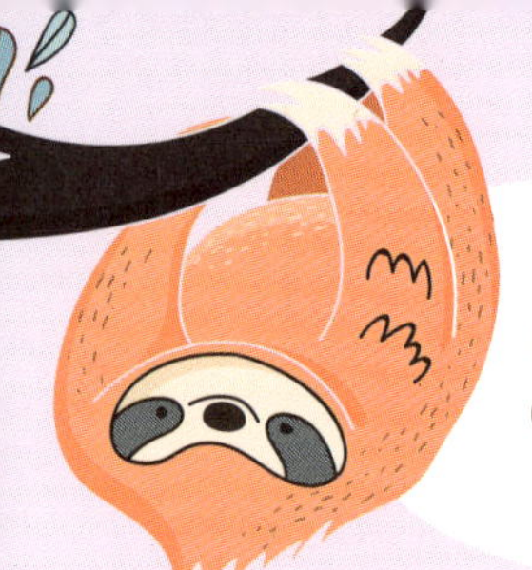

Sleep-o-Meter

**I slept really well all through the night,
I woke up with a smile, everything feeling just right.**

Write about your joyful morning after a pleasant night's sleep.

____

____

____

____

____

____

____

____

____

____

____

____

I didn't sleep well through the night,
I woke up with a frown, not feeling right.

Draw your sleepy morning face. Remember it is okay to not feel okay.

Memory Box

- Find a special box.
- Gather things that make you happy.
- Pick five favorites for little siblings.
- Place items inside.
- Tape the box shut.
- Ask for help to protect it.

What have you kept inside the box?
When do you plan to open it? And with whom?

Wishful Approvals

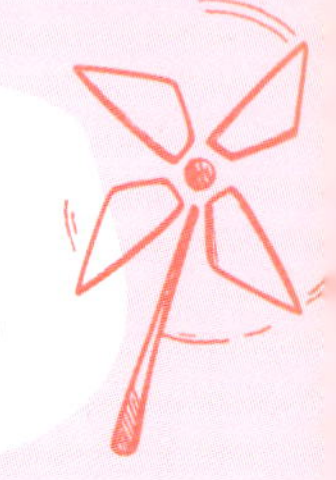

My grown-ups are in YES-DAY mode. They will cheerfully say yes to every wish I make.

The delightful things I would ask for are:

Joyful Creations

I am a super-duper artist.
Here are some of my cool mindful creations.

Bunny hops, superstar!

Sunflower smiles, wow!

Dreams delight!

Panda's pride!

Sweet toffee, yum!

Little bolt, big love!

Kite flies high, congrats!

Friendship blooms!

Draw happy stickers to match each phrase.

'Outer Me'

My joyful expression to the world.

'Inner Me'
My feelings and thoughts within me.

Express your happiness on the 'Outer Me' side and share your feelings and thoughts on the 'Inner Me' side. Draw or write.

Tweeting Peace

Silent dove, up I glide,
Peace, I sow far and wide.
Share love, not spite,
Feel calm while you color
me bright.

PEACE

Simon Says

Winking my eyes, twirling around, hopping right and left, giving my hands a shake, enjoying a playful twist, and waving a warm hello.

I have followed Simon's lead so far. Now, I wonder, what might Simon's next command be.

On a rainy day:

For quick classroom activity:

Take with you on a trip:

For sleepover fun:

Family game night:

Break the ice with:

Be Your Own Cheerleader

Words can guide, dreams inside.
Repeat affirmations, that's where I will abide.
I write my favorite,
planting dreams deep and wide.

Say kind words to yourself, repeat them, and write them down for a happiness boost.

Thank You, Every Day

When I am thankful for what I have got,
I find joy in every little spot.

Consider all the things you are thankful for. Each time you feel grateful, write 'thank you.' Keep adding these little gems of gratitude to your life.